THE

DRUNKEN

DRIVER

HAS THE

RIGHT

OF WAY

THE

DRUNKEN

DRIVER

HAS THE

RIGHT

OF WAY

poems

ETHAN
COEN

 CROWN PUBLISHERS / NEW YORK

Published by Crown Publishers, New York, New York.
Member of the Crown Publishing Group.

Random House, Inc. New York, Toronto, London, Sydney, Auckland
www.randomhouse.com

CROWN is a trademark and the Crown colophon is a registered
trademark of Random House, Inc.

Printed in the United States of America

DESIGN BY KAREN MINSTER

Library of Congress Cataloging-in-Publication Data
Coen, Ethan
The drunken driver has the right of way : poems / by Ethan Coen.
p.cm. I. Title. PS3553.O348 D78 2001 811'.54—dc21 2001028240
ISBN 0-609-60946-7

10   9   8   7   6   5   4   3   2   1

First Edition

CONTENTS

THE

DRUNKEN

DRIVER

HAS THE

RIGHT

OF WAY

"MR. SANDS"

He had an accent, "Mr. Sands;"
Was fond of wearing four-in-hands;
His friends, like him from parts unknown,
Wore four-in-hands much like his own.

They'd jabber loudly in his room
But mumly smile at lodgers whom
They'd genuflect past on the stair;
Some had soup stains on their neckwear.

Our Mr. Sands was neat at tea
But, finished, he'd rise instantly
And bow, adjusting his cravat,
Then fly up to his third-floor flat.

He puttered quite a bit up there.
He'd much the neatest facial hair
Of any roomer; we surmised
That that absorbed him, or his ties.

We left him to his own affairs
Until the bomb blew up upstairs.
We tie his ties now; Mr. Sands
Cannot knot knots, not having hands.

TO O

O!
I love a poem that starts with an O!
For it is a vigorous thing.
From a deeply felt spring
It must spring, and you know
That its rhymes all will ring
And its rhythms will flow;
O's the cap of the heart's highest swells;
How its spirit infects us;
It punches the plexus
And grabs the lapels;
It's a cri from the couer,
It's a shout down the hall;
O you vocative yoo-hoo,
Muse-summoning bawl;
Quel kick in the kishkes,
What stomp-upon-toe,
What welling of joy
Or of bone-crushing woe,
What feeling, what fuoco,
What brio-to-be-O
Foretokens inaugural O!

O!
I love a poet who uses an O!
He visits Parnassian heights.
His mental lips pucker
Round thoughts that he chews;
I'm always a sucker
For words he may favor
And tropes he may use;
I'm certain to savor
With ohs, ahs and oohs

The phrases he forms; his
Faux pas I'll excuse,
Infelicities wink at
And lapses I'll choose
To ignore, for his don't's are
The price of his do's;
That poet
Must know what
Is what who
Can't but through
His poem
Strew O, him
Who must, will, and does utter O!
　Mighty O!
That grandly ejaculate
　Literato,
The poet who uses an O!

O!
I love a poem that ends with an O!
It leaves with its head held up high;
It gives us an orotund
Heave and a ho
Out into the echoing
Silenzio
That follows the ultimate O,
　Mighty O!
The grand valedictory
Terminal, germinal
Bay of the heart
That debuted and'll part
As the belle of verse ball and
The star of our show;
O long may abound

O; long may O be found
Ending verse, for I'm ape
For that marvelous sound
And that middleless shape
That all smoke-ringers blow, that
Lip-leaver-agape
That I know you now know;
With a one for the money
And two for the show
And a last valedic—
And away we all go
With a wave o' the hand
And a tilt of chapeau;
Here's the end that was planned
From the word go, and so
Adios, au revoir, toodle-oo, adio,
I sign off with the letter
Than which none is better
For how could this poem
Be ended but so
When all verse with deep-seated
Respect for repeated
O-use is completed
By (anything else would be inapropos
For a poem that celebrates O!)
An O!
So here alas is a last
O which I shan't go past—
This, thus, the unsurpassed O:
O!

That was the very last O!

THE DRUNKEN DRIVER HAS
THE RIGHT OF WAY

The loudest have the final say,
The wanton win, the rash hold sway,
The realist's rules of order say
The drunken driver has the right of way.

The Kubla Khan can butt in line;
The biggest brute can take what's mine;
When heavyweights break wind, that's fine;
No matter what a judge might say,
The drunken driver has the right of way.

The guiltiest feel free of guilt;
Who care not, bloom; who worry, wilt;
Plans better laid are rarely built
For forethought seldom wins the day;
The drunken driver has the right of way.

The most attentive and unfailing
Carefulness is unavailing
Wheresoever fools are flailing;
Wisdom there is held at bay;
The drunken driver has the right of way.

De jure is de facto's slave;
The most foolhardy beat the brave;
Brass routs restraint; low lies high's grave;
When conscience leads you, it's astray;
The drunken driver has the right of way.

It's only the naivest who'll
Deny this, that the reckless rule;
When facing an oncoming fool
The practiced and sagacious say
Watch out—one side—look sharp—gang way.

However much you plan and pray,
Alas, alack, *tant pis, oy we,*
Now—heretofore—'til Judgment Day,
The drunken driver has the right of way.

TALE OF THE YUKON

Hit icehole mushing thrash and climb
Out kindled fire not in time
Feet froze sled sunk no walk no ride
He ate his sled dogs then he died.

ON DAVEY JONES

The sea it resembles a tippling bore
That is loath to let you go;
It embraces you with a drunken tug
And vomits brine and nameless crud.

It pounds and roars and thumps its chest
    And vomits brine and nameless crud.

Aye, it vomits brine and nameless crud.

A bore, a boor, without manners or grace,
    The sea has a changeable mood;
It'll silently sulk and then tipsily race,
    Then, again, much like he who is stewed,
Will in sudden exhaustion fall flat on its face
    And'll snore in dead calm interlude.

                                So,
The sea, laddies, is the place for me, oh!
A seafaring seadog am I!
And when this heart no longer thumps,
A salty seagoing sailor's grave,
A saline grave, a sailing grave,
With coffin of current and headstone of wave,
Yes, a saline grave want I!

                                Aye,
My lubbering corpse will eternally rest
On the breast of mi madre la mer,
And I'll feed them that dwell in the primeval soup—
    Aye, I'll batten and fatten the 'cetti and shark;
    I'll lie fast 'neath the hatches of 'cetti and shark;

I'll be stokin' the engines of 'cetti and shark—
And no more bestride orlop nor poop!

And no windlass and davit line will from the deep
Upgesück me—and nor'll yon hawsers.
As the flying fish fly and the blue narwhals bound
Past the 'cetti and shark within which I'll be found
    Concommingled with former co-seagoing mates
      And with brit and John Dory and grouper
          and skates
       And with brine and nameless crud,
I'll sleep sound!

So it's lively, lads! O'er the rail with me! Those
That's left, pickle your gullets with grog!
Once I sets down me scrimshaw and turns up
    me toes
Mind ye pitch me out into the vagues!

For the sea it resembles a bibulous bore
Whose embrace is insistent and strong!
In the bellies of both juices roil and churn
And they bubble and slosh from the stem to
    the stern
And yet I through my spyglass a difference discern—
    Aye, I one thing most markedly mark:
Insofar as is known, parmacetti and shark
Dwelleth not in the bellies of sots,
Which is why when my seafaring sea-carcass rots
Feed me not to a bibulous—
    Please when I plotz—
Feed me not to a bibu—when
    My bilge pump stops—

Feed me not to a bibulous—
    Never a bibulous—
Nary a bibulous—
    Please, I implore!—
Feed me not to a bibulous bore,
    Bore, bore;
If you please, not a bibulous bore!

FOR WHAT IT'S WORTH

If you can count your complement
Of digits up to twenty
You could give a toe or finger to
A friend, and still have plenty.

You could even lend an ear to an
Unfortunate with none,
But by no means hand out noses since
Of those you have but one.

No no-nose should fault you for your
Hoarding your more to his fewer,
For your gift would make what's true of
Him of you as true, or truer.

Just remind him his anasalness
Is the estate *he* chose
On that day when someone said to *him*,
"I have a need of nose."

No no, Goodness knows no folly and
No wastrel knows the Good;
Hand out your nose and naught'll be
Right where your nose be should.

So act the lord with fingers and
Play fast and loose with toes,
But remember to remember,
Be tightfisted with your nose.

ANTHROPOLOGY

What sort of people would you guess
Once farmed these plains? One seeks a sign.
Their homes proclaim their humbleness;
Behind each house, a simple shrine

Bespeaks their piety. What god
Or goddess ruled this chapel poor,
The way to which is so well trod?
—Selene, judging by the door.

OLD AGE

I put on my own drawers today,
And which is more than some can say,
And ventured out of doors today—
    Hurrah, my boys, hurrah!

I had a solid nap today,
And which is more than some can say,
And, during, did not crap today—
    Hurrah, my boys, hurrah!

I had a lucid thought today,
And which is more than some can say;
My fleeing wits I caught today—
    Hurrah, my boys, hurrah!

My bowels moved quite well today,
And which is more than some can say;
They trundled out and fell today—
    Hurrah, my boys, hurrah!

My wife's words went unsaid today,
And which is more than some can say,
For she remained long-dead today—
    Hurrah, my boys, hurrah!

My pleasures were clear-cut today,
And which is more than some can say;
Youth worries; Age has but today—
    Hurrah, my boys,
    Hurrah hurrah!
Though some say wipe your chin, I say
    Hurrah, my boys, hurrah!

HORNS

If my wit were keener, so it
Could in stubborn language carve
My love's likeness, then a poet
I would be—and we would starve.

Lacking art to match my ardor
I'm not sure what to bemoan
As I drudge to stock the larder,
For my love weighs thirteen stone.

Which is which, o sword, if one edge
Cuts for good and one for ill?
Is my lover cursed with tonnage?
Spared a lover's pointless skill?

Do regrets prick more the poet
Or the dullard? Her shape so,
Should I even wish to show it
In a verbal cameo?

AFTER BUKOWSKI

Mao was constipated.
Sometimes they had to reach in
To pull out the Chairman's stool.
Jesus,
What a job.
Mentally,
He was not constipated.
The Cultural Revolution.
He thought that one up.
Maybe his wife helped.

With the Cultural Revolution, I mean.

Jesus.

SUCH SWEET SORROW

If there were times
I slighted you
I'm sorry now
    There weren't more.

So many times
I fought with you
But, sadly, never
    Broke your jaw.

Some days, I know,
I failed to show
    You what you meant to me,

However it
Is hard to hit
    That hard that frequently.

I wanted wine and roses and
You gave me marcs and thorns,
And also marks of black and blue
And shiny cuckold's horns.

I do regret
The way I let
    You always get my goat,

But don't repent
The time I spent
    With hands wrapped round your throat.

I would have loved your laughter
Were it not at my expense,
And hope you will hereafter
Be amused by hell's torments.

So should we meet
Upon the street
 You should know why, instead

Of hailing you
With love, I do
 So with a hail of lead.

C. DARWIN

If C. saw Providence contrive
To doom a trait that wouldn't do,
Then how'd Improvidence survive
When no one knew what Noah knew?

THREE PLACES

I. On Not Seeing the Taj Mahal by Moonlight

I haven't visited the Taj,
    Nor do most poets care to.
Mahal rhymes little; ditto Taj;
    Ergo whyfore go thereto?

II. On Big Bear Lake

High-sloshing midst the ruggedy
    San Bernardino Mountains
Lies Lake Big Bear—and this is where
    My brief Big Bear account ends.

III. In Chi We Lod

Chicago is a beefy place
    Of shoulders broad and vowels odd
Whose pinnacles' skyscraping grace
    Her sons would say all men applod.

Her Board of Trade, her El, her Loop
    Which throngs each day with men aplod,
Her winds, which leave the lake aswoop,
    Leave tourists awed and natives odd.

Her sights, her smells, her sounds, her speech
    Grown flat upon her native sod,
Her Poles, her blacks, her blues clubs—each
    We'd elsewhere laud; in Chi we lod.

AGENT ELEGY

No more will the Russian Tea Room
Find him hailing every friend,
Holding forth on points, per diem,
Fee, breakeven and back end.

He will dine no more at Morton's
Nor press flesh while trade is chatted,
For his own flesh would slough off now
Were hands shaken or backs patted.

His teeth tear no more at blini,
His eyes brim no more with greed,
His hands clutch no more at ten percent,
His heart still doesn't beat.

Now he wears but one Italian suit
Of ever looser fit,
And his smile, once conferred on few,
Now's indiscriminate.

Smooth, the brow once knit with scheming;
Spent, the double-dealing hours;
He's serene, and even spritely,
Now that he sprouts wildflowers.

Though, for most, corruption follows
Death, for him it went before;
Hold his calls, and mark his headstone,
"Incorrupt, forevermore."

THE HOPPING POEM

Fuck
Fuck
Fuck
Fuck,

That
Hurt,
Fuck
Fuck.

THE FABLE OF C. EDGAR BOTTS

There once was a young lad named C. Edgar Botts
Who wore eyes in glasses and bow ties in knots;
He pulled up girls' pigtails and down their culottes,
For such a young lad was young C. Edgar Botts.

Young Edgar would, rather than playing with friends,
Incinerate ants with his spectacle lens
Or smash the glass turtles on Auntie's whatnots,
For such a young lad was young C. Edgar Botts.

He threw stones at pigeons and tree toads at girls,
Chased titmice with hammers, laid poison for squirrels;
He flattered the bigger boys and beat the tots,
For such a young lad was young C. Edgar Botts.

A boy down the way who was named Bertram Sayles
Saw C. Edgar tie empty tins to cats' tails;
He grabbed him and, though Edgar whinnied
    and shrieked,
He beat him 'til Edgar's eyes ran and nose leaked,

And warned Edgar that if he'd not had his fill
Of naughtiness, next time would go harder still.
And so, plus fours mussed and his waistcoat in spots,
Back home to his mummy ran C. Edgar Botts.

    Moral for all young boys:

Whenever you're roaming about of a day
And doing those things that lads do when at play,
Keep rocks in your pockets and mind you look out
In case there are bullies like Bertram about.

I LOVE YOU DEEPLY, DARLING

If all geniuses were shallow
And if dullards all were deep,
And our waking lives were but
Somebody's dreams who couldn't sleep,

And all nonsense bore repeating
And repeating didn't bore,
I would love you yet, and say so
Many times times many more.

And if all the world ran backwards
I would love you deeply still,
'Til the rivers ran downriver
And the mountains ran uphill.

Yes, I love you to the point where
Logic and illogic meet,
And adduce as proof these sentiments
Regarding you, my sweet:

If subjunctives were, in fact, and
Counterfactuals could be;
Hypotheticals did happen,
Say; conditionals ran free,

And the straight lines went all wavy,
And the circles hunkered square,
And if milquetoasts went out roistering
When rowdies didn't dare,

Still I'd love you, sure as A is A
And long as B is B—
Longer still, should they suspend the
Laws of self-identity.

Should *that* happen I would yet know
Certain certain certainties:
A) That B could then be not-B;
B) That B's could then be C's;

C) I'd know that I'd still love you
Even when I wasn't me;
Whom I then was would no doubt be
Too confused to disagree.

So if—given that all me's would have
My present attitude—
These subjunctives are indicative,
I'll never change my mood.

Aye, my love's ad infinitum;
Ab initio as well;
As ad hominem as always,
Thou dear dearest dear, thou swell;

I outlove all if's that are, were,
Might be, and that aren't, too,
For I love you as I'd love you
If I loved you as I do.

And I love you madly, madly,
Past the point of making sense,
And I offer the foregoing
In the way of evidence.

Yes I love you deeply, darling,
But if depth leaves you perplexed,
This tractatus I retract and
Shall try shallow trifles next.

MY DREAM AND
WHAT I MAKE OF IT

Part One: My Dream

In my dream last night I was a toucan
With a nose that was hard as a shell,
   So I rapped knuckles on it,
   Cracked walnuts upon it,
And cashews and filberts as well.

Yes, I cracked open walnuts upon it,
And used it to bang at my bell.

   Yes, I ate walnut meat
   While my two toucan feet
Took turns standing. The nightcloth then fell.

So I went down the hall to the kitchen
Where I put up the water for tea.
   Little bubbles ascended
   And popped unattended,
Then wended their way to the sea.

The tea bubbled and seethed unattended
Until just before fifty to three.

   When its bubbles dispersed
   The tea picked up its purse
And it took the 2:10 to the sea.

So I sailed to the white cliffs of Dover,
But they had a chalk undertaste when
   I spread them on scones
   After sifting their stones,
As you must, or your gut'll distend.

You must pick out the rocks
To avoid aftershocks
The next day when they leave your rear end.

And so that was my dream and my journey,
And I fondly recall those days when
I would sail up and down and
Asea and aground and
Have never been heard from again.

Oh, I sailed seven seas
And earned eight Ph.D.'s
And won nine games of euchre in ten,

But my luck and degrees
(And advanced gum disease)
Wound up alienating my men.

So the great waves beneath
Which reposed all my teeth
Bore me back to reflect
In mature retrospect
On the unparalleled
Nose I'd had and nuts shelled
And tea brewed and scones eaten
And grog taken neat and
The wonderful places I'd been.

Part Two: What I Make of It

There are days I still like to go sailing,
And days when I like to stay put,
    So some days I roam and
    Some others stay home and
Still others I seafare by foot.

    I put on galoshes
    To keep out the sloshes
And then I go sailing on foot.

There are days when I act like a grown-up,
Although fortunately they are rare,
    For I usually dream and
    Eat cake and ice cream and
Imagine whatever's not there.

    What is real isn't fertile
    For me, though dessert'll
Be that for which I'll always care.

There are those who think I should be working,
But unhappily I have a quirk:
    What will happen, alas, is
    My urge to work passes
Before it can pass into work.

    Let my good friends the masses
    Get up off their asses
While I stay at home with a smirk.

Although many believe work ennobles,
Others don't, and among them is me.
    My behind, as if leaden,
    Lies anchored in bed in
A languor and I disagree

With whomever finds indolence shameful;
Conscientiousness makes me berserk:
    Whatsoever the task is
    All ever I'll ask is,
Is there any way I can shirk?

    Loafing leaves me content,
    Though your diligent gent
    Might regard me as some kind of
    (Some kind of (some kind of
    (Some kind of (some kind of))))
Jerk.

So I nap and take naps and lie napping,
And then in between sometimes I doze,
    Although sometimes I'll deign
    To write something inane
Just to keep the old head on its toes.

    On occasion I'll scribble
    A frip or a fribble
Or merest petite quelque chose.

Part Three: Conclusion

From my dream flows my code of behavior,
And without which no man is complete,
    For one's life is misspent
    Without firm fundament
To recline on while resting one's feet,

    So ignore that injunction
    That bids a man function
In otherwise than stockinged feet.

No enlightened soul harbors ambition;
Who advance not need never retreat;
    Whom the urge to act stirs
    Ineluctably errs;
Without effort, there's never defeat;

    Ergo act as if, not
    Just the credo you've got,
But you too, have been set in concrete.

BACK WHEN THE WORLD WAS
FRESH AND NEW

Back when the world was fresh and new,
    Before Man trod upon it,
God, thinking final touches through,
    Envisioned sod upon it.

With green side up and care supreme,
    And without stint of trouble,
Laid sod the Lord, and smoothed each seam,
    And stamped out every bubble.

'Til raking time lord God was pleased;
    A changeless autumn's prodding
Bethought Him then, though, of the trees
    He'd left beneath His sodding.

The One, with furtive glance and keen,
    Checked if He was alone or
If anyone about had seen
    That He had pulled a boner.

Thus reassured none would be heard
    Deriding the Almighty,
The Highest High Himself bestirred
    To cure the oversight. He

Rolled up and stacked the soddy rolls
    And with great pulls and pushes
Hove up the trees, and heaped their holes
    With dirt. Likewise, the bushes.

He then relaid the sod; upon
    It, reaffixed the flora;
The tale He banned from Myth, Upan-
    ishad, Koran, and Torah.

LIMERICKS

In a much-scribbled privy in Wald
I once read and was greatly appalled
By this verse. Though it scanned,
I still can't understand
How, why, when, or by whom it was scrawled.

~~~

A Scot lingering in a cold shower
Saw that those which he'd soaped for an hour
Had retreated and shrunk
In a whiskery funk
Like a fieldmouse turned up by a plower.

~~~

"Throw from ten paces in that direction
Without banking them off my mid-section;
I'll scream *'Merci beaucoup'*
After every time you
Land an onion ring on my erection."

~~~

She worked out every day at the Y
And cracked walnuts with levering thigh.
All her beaus would complain
Of a great ringing pain
In their ears after kissing goodbye.

~~~

Once a rhino with drives so voracious
And with genitals so ostentatious
That all she-rhinos shrank
Eyed an old Sherman tank
In a manner distinctly salacious.

~

Wine glass raised to the wife of his host,
A guest offered the following toast:
"To a friend of all here,
With one failing, I fear—
Or we all have been misdiagnosed."

~

In the bed of the raj of Darjeeling
Lay a stool which, although unappealing,
Still did not disturb some
Near as much as the come
Clinging glutinously to the ceiling.

~

A man torn between lusts and pretensions
Bought a brothel but ringed it with gentians
And in it threw fêtes
At which leggy brunettes
Performed giggling Latin declensions.

~

When her flatulence grew unabating
Gwen bemoaned its effect upon mating:
"Though beaus used to abound
And grow firm I have found
That a ripsawlike sound is deflating."

⁓

It was *his* estate now, so the heir
Humped a sapling-hole under the stare
Of the gardener, Juan,
Who cried "*¡Oiga!* Come on,
Cutty doubt pudding peepee in dare!"

⁓

While pretending to use his tea towel
The uncomfortable hostess hissed, "Howell,
If I can't quell this fart
Clap a hand to your heart
And cry out, 'Hallo, there's the old bowel!' "

"If my duties allowed," he demurred,
"But the lord and I just had a word
And he asked if, by chance,
Once he'd felt through his pants,
I might step out to chuck a small turd."

Staff in my day—mind, times were less slack—
Ruddy well never answered you back.
At a lady's behest a
Chap juggled egesta
And gas, or was given the sack.

⁓

A hillbilly tip: "My paw knowed
How to diddle a squirrel and showed
Me the way it-all's done:
'Wrap some tape round 'er, son,
Or the critter'll up'n explode.' "

We'd informed them how Father Hart—who'd
Guzzle sherry and, after he'd spewed,
Would hold forth in his undies—
On balmier Sundays
Administered mass in the nude;

Well, he said as they led him away
He'd return on a real Judgment Day
And the altar boys screw,
And the crèche Virgin, too,
Even if she *was* papier-mâché,

So we pray for him now, and our chief
Hope is that he regain his belief,
But all night and all day
By the Christmas display
Stands a guard whom we've armed to the teeth.

So efficient was Nell with her twat
That a line formed, and moved at a trot.
One man, gasping and red,
Called her very ill-bred
But refused to relinquish his spot.

Overheard in a house of correction:
"Kid, it was too an act of affection,
Otherwise I could well
Have complained of the smell
And could not have maintained my erection."

~◞

Judge not: Yes, there are those who insert
Their own amative parts in a yurt;
Yes, with pleasure their peepees
Probe conical teepees
And pup tents which strike them as pert,

But, pray, is it "perverse" to love tents?
One who'd sneered at such "abnormal" bents
Entertained quite a class
Of odd things up his ass
And proposed to a white picket fence.

~◞

As the last of the firelight flickers,
Brandy chinks on its tray, and the vicar's
Maid, quaking in place,
Murmurs, "Sorry, Your Grace;
I'm c-cold when you wear my kn-knickers."

~◞

The artiste garnered barely a glance
And but carping as thanks for her dance,
One man grousing a pastie
Had not been as tasty
Or moist as her lace underpants.

～

A young man who fucks knotholes in trees
Says revenge is his reason, and he's
Had relations with shrubs
Since the best garden clubs
Snubbed his purple and pink peonies.

Be he victim or vandal or sleaze,
He ignores Pete the Park Ranger's pleas:
Not to put on a condom,
Pete says, is beyond him
These days what with Dutch elm disease.

～

All the nursing home's old wisenheimers
Became glum in the grip of Alzheimer's.
Puzzled silence would fall
When one tried to recall
The next line of a favorite one-liner.

～

Farmer Jones knew his neighbor McNee
Much admired his paint mare but he
Was still stunned when he tendered
A bill—"Having rendered
Stud services personally."

~⌍

Awkward youth! He loved Carmen Miranda
But the walls of the studio and a
Guard's sneering rebuff
Sent him home in a huff
Where he wept as he humped his stuffed panda.

~⌍

A tumultuous standing ovation
Met the life science don's declaration
That "How Young Are Begot"
Was to be covered not
By a lecture, but live demonstration.

~⌍

Speak, young belle! "Now with beaus,
    your best course is
Drub their penis, which right there enforces
Your whim. When Bud calls?
Daddy batters his balls—
But that's beatin' a team a dead horses.

"Like when main him'll park I might say,
'Bud, beefhour we go all away?
I done just set my hair,
Both on top a noun air;
Now, you muss it, LB Hellapay!' "

An inscrutable Chinaman, Ping,
Gravely taught his own penis to sing.
During sex his wife, Wong,
Gravely mumbled along
When she heard muffled bebop and swing.

Benedetto "Ol' Freethinkin' " Croce
Little feared, late in life, death's approach. He
Largely stuck to his guns,
Yelling "Numbnuts!" at nuns;
"God? *What* God?" though, now came sotto voce.

Camembert, like all runnier cheeses,
Brings to mind the ejecta of sneezes,
And yet some like its taste
Like their own solid waste;
One man's *merda* another man's meat is.

While fellating the fifth earl of Kent
The head butler began to relent:
"Good my lord, by your schlong
You've your lineage wrong,
For the fourth and third earls' weren't bent."

～つ

The indignant man's waiter was sure he
Could explain the fresh come in the curry:
"See, the pastry chef, Kurt,
Jisms on the dessert,
But today he's in some kind of hurry."

～つ

There was once a good Catholic who
Stuck a rosary up his wazoo
By means of which fairies
Could count the Hail Marys
They thereby obliged him to do.

～つ

The old farmer's wife only objects
To her man's extramarital sex
When he pulls down his drawers
And performs it outdoors,
With the chickens, while wringing their necks.

～つ

As new chief the Pawnee would promote him
Who could lift the tribe's heaviest totem.
While he served, it would swing
From his balls by a string.
Former chiefs were called Men of Great Scrotum.

A philatelist out in the sticks
Had to patiently tell all the hicks
Who had offered to sit
For philately, it
In fact wasn't the sucking of dicks.

Without pockets, a drunk in Belfast
Took to socking his change up his ass.
He'd moon barmaids and men
And say, "Watch and say when
I have paid out the price of a Bass."

In the dark, the girl's innocent chum
Misdirected his dick up her bum.
Being told gently so,
The lad piped, "Penis? No!
This is how I've stopped sucking my thumb!"

A gourmand speaks to those who decry
His chef d'ouevre, an excrement pie:
"While I wouldn't dispute
That it's soupy *en croute,*
By itself it bakes terribly dry."

∿

It is Freedom of Speech, the courts say,
And the zoo thus cannot dock the pay
Of the keeper whose howls
While screwing the owls
Was scaring the children away.

∿

From a text found in old Turkestan:
"List for love between camel and man:
Taffy—two pounds at least,
For distracting the beast;
Stable stepladder; getaway plan."

∿

There are crones on the streets of Algiers
Who tell fortunes by means of their rears.
Luck in Love is one fart,
Two predicts Broken Heart;
Spattered shit just means free souvenirs.

∿

Hamsters doggedly seek to instruct
By example how humans are fucked:
Upon wheels they can't climb
They run only through time
On fast-forward to auto-destruct.

~

So excited at movies was Lou,
His own penis impeded his view.
When he nudged it aside
An irked girl in back cried,
"Could the bald guy not bob fro and to!"

~

Ed received, as he's keen to relate,
Oral sex from an eighty-pound skate.
Though his friends stand him drinks
Not a one of them thinks
That that actually was the thing's weight.

~

Brother Vladimir couldn't but bristle
To see fresh-coiled shit on his missal.
He said, hunched on a cassock
Of Patriarch Vlasic,
"If *that* made him laugh, maybe *this*'ll."

~

"Higher function," reflects an old hag,
"Is in retrospect rather a drag.
Other folks used to not
Spoon my food, stanch my snot,
Or replace my colostomy bag."

Upon Asia's high, timberless tracts
Lonely herdsmen, in time, must face facts:
Though they sowed wild oats
With the nimblest goats,
Age demotes them to union with yaks.

Grace grew listless and ate more and more
'Til her clients her favors foreswore,
Voicing doubts about Grace
And their penises' place
In so vast and indifferent a whore.

The devices that Dolly employed
Only literally filled the void
That no man could quite plumb—
Though, of those who tried, some
Reconnoitered in ways she enjoyed.

" 'Cat,' " he said at the bar. "Really. Is
That for Kathrine, Miss? —Mrs.? Uh . . . Ms.?"
She blinked blankly at him,
Lifted one lazy limb,
Licked her privates, and trod upon his.

To the high lamasery Bob climbed
Whose monks bade him unfetter his mind
By imbibing the rich
Sudsy yak urine which
They themselves had with giggles declined.

She did not date in Early Cretaceous,
Being spikey, cold-blooded, pugnacious;
And then how many males
Go for vulva with scales
And vaginas so clammy and spacious?

Ahmet doubly paid as a prude
When his intimates came to collude
So that in the chador
He had bought for his whore
Was his wife, whom he guiltily screwed.

Soirée finished at Golden Age Courts,
Frankel pondered the freight in his shorts:
"Though I held my ass tight
In the slow dance, I might
Have relaxed when I dipped Mrs. Schwartz."

Pete informed the divorcée from Boise
Who'd proved passionate but rather noisy,
Screaming just as she came
Her ex-husband's pet name,
"Ma'am, just here, reminiscence annoys me."

But the gloom the encounter created
Only grew with the next girl he dated
Who, on losing control,
Shrieked the Elk Lodge's roll,
Then moaned Moose as her passion abated.

He took up with a woman from Butte
Not the least because she was a mute,
But while holding her knees
Her hands named attendees
Of a house of uncertain repute.

Lord, one hopes that he won't come to know
That for her Cupid metered his bow.
Her love's dumb—keep his blind;
Some sow salt if they find
Any dirt where they've plowed a new row.

MORE LIMERICKS:
SONS OF ABRAHAM

A rich bedouin from Abu Dhabi
Jerked his Thoroughbreds off as a hobby,
Though he sometimes instead
Gave his old camel head
Just to show that he hadn't grown snobby.

His great-uncle, a sheik of Qatar,
Picked up boys in his Cadillac car
And kept stowed in its trunk
Dog-eared copies of *Hunk*,
Vaseline, and a toy scimitar.

The sheik's friend, an emir of Oman,
Kept a swing band outside of his john
Which would play, when he sat,
"String of Pearls" 'til he shat,
And "The King Porter Stomp" thereupon.

These men ridiculed Rabbi Yablans
Who, constrained by strict doctrinal bonds,
Would have sex with prayer shawls
Coyly cloaking his balls
And phylacteries wrapped round his schwanz.

Can't these Semites be friends just as some
Even less likely folk have become?
Grant met Lee, after all;
Berlin toppled its wall,
And King Oedipus loved his own mum.

WHAT, THEN, IS THE POINT?
CLEAN LIMERICKS

There was once a gelatinous blob
Which could not, lacking handle or knob,
Be picked up, put away,
Made to move, made to stay,
Or do other than jiggle and bob.

~

A recidivist sent to San Quentin,
Despite seven-to-ten to repent in,
Said, "It's like any hitch—
An impertinence which
I resent having had no assent in.

"Though I never owned autos, nor went in
Search of Easter eggs, my life's been spent in
Making tin license plates
In twelve pens in ten states
And cane baskets from Chino to Trenton."

~

A half-stewed elocutionist trod
On a bartop and, fanning a wad,
Bellowed "All this goes to
Whomsoever of you
Can pronounce in one syllable 'Gstaad.' "

~

Bob Ampudia had quite a gut,
But with wheelbarrow serving as strut
He could move it about—
Though it sometimes slopped out
And slammed into his knees at a rut.

REUNION

Say! You look great!
    Well, *you* look great!
We *both* look great—
How long's it been?
    How long's it been?—
    A long, long time.
A long, long time.
    Well, you look great!

Al

Have you seen Al?
    No—Al is here?
Yeah, Al is here.
    So, how's Al look?
Al looks real good.
    And how's Al been?
Al shot his wife.
    . . . But how's *Al* been?

Sid

Did you see Sid?
    I did see Sid.
Heh—same old Sid.
    Yeah, Sid is Sid.
Boy, that guy Sid.
    Sid, boy oh boy.
Sid—hah hah hah.
    Hah hah hah—Sid.

Eileen

Seen Eileen Walsh?
    Who's Eileen Walsh?
Eileen *Pierce* Walsh?
    Oh—Eileen *Pierce*!
Yeah, Eileen Pierce.
    I *fucked* Eileen!
You fucked *Eileen*?
    Huh! Eileen *Walsh*?

Herman Frank

There's Herman Frank.
    That's Herman Frank?!—
    Say, he's lost weight!
No—over there.
    Whu—*oh* my *God*!
Yeah. Pretty sad.
    He's *put on* weight!
Yeah, and he's—Herm!

        Hi Joe! Hi Ed!
    Herm!
Herm!
        Hey ho!
    Herm, how you been?
        I can't complain;
        Still get around—
        Just need these canes.
Well, you look great!
    You two do too!

Irv

There's Irv—the dork.
    He made some dough.
Yeah, so I heard,
But still a—geez!
Is that his date?
    No, that's his wife.
That young one?! Her
With the, uh, tits?

Leaving

    Well, au revoir.
We'll owe Irv what?
    No—*au revoir.*
Oh—au revoir.
    Yeah. Keep in touch.
Yeah. Keep in touch.

God, what a putz.

    God, what a putz.

Now those are tits!

A NAUGHTY VERSE

There are many ways to signal
To your guests that dinner's through:
Serving mints, inviting speeches,
Or just vomiting'll do.

Although least genteel, the last of these
Is favored most by me;
It foments post-prandial mirth
And fairly reeks of *sans souci,*

For, like any act impromptu,
Its gay, unforced air is cheering;
Too, it empties out the dining room
So servants can start clearing.

It'll cut short expeditiously
A long and boring toast,
Or may put at ease the awkward guest
Now suaver than his host;

It's a source of conversation
Over snifters and cigars,
And's remembered past the humdrum rounds
Of snooker, draughts and cards;

It can serve as wordless hint to all
That time is growing late,
Or may serve as retrospective of
The meal that all just ate.

Yes, it's quite the thing, and guaranteed
To put your neighborhood on
Notice that within your portals
Ceremony isn't stood on.

So when, cummerbunds undone, all
Sigh in languor and await
Evening's final rumination,
Offer yours—regurgitate!

IS THIS THING ON?

Hello. Hello.
Is this thing on?
Is this thing on?
Hello. Hello.

One two three four
Five six. Hello.
Is this thing on?
Hello. Hello.

NEVER-ENDING REMEMBRANCE

I have wandered ancient alleys in a city by the sea
And have slipped upon the cobblestones and bruised
   my buttocks three
For I have a spare that I take care to carry there
   with me
Should a cobblestone upend me in a city by the sea.

It was misty musings brought me to that city by
   the sea
In the wistful season after she had died who was
   to me
More an angel than an angel ever would in modesty
Claim to equal as an angel, though so mortal—
   Oh!—proved she.

It was grief! and loss! and heartache! brought me to
   that seaside we
Had upon a time once visited when we had seemed
   to be
Full of future! spreading future! rising, rising,
   endlessly!
—For its dizzy drops and dismal stops we two could
   not foresee.

Oh, how my young bride was happy ere contracting
   the TB
That precluded sleep—nor hers alone; her hacking
   soon sent me
Out of doors upon walks-ruminant; a muse I
   hunted—she,
Dark-eyed Dolour, who made Edgar Allan Poe try
   poetry.

And my soul I christened LAMMERMOOR,
    which rang poetically,
And my pale bride AEGIUS I dubbed, though she
    was not a he,
And my derriere I opted to denominate HENRI,
But my inspiration ended there; no poems came
    to me.

And when my bride died the seraphs sighed and
    sunlight ceased to be
In the shuttered chambers of my heart wherein,
    sepulchrally,
Echoes echoed, yet no sound nor its rebound
    distracted me
From my morbid contemplations and dilations
    on ennui.

And of nights I haunted public houses
    LAMMERMOORFULLY
And bewailed my AEGIUS's fate with so
    much energy
That at customers' request I was ejected bodily,
Whereupon upon the sidewalk I'd alight
    upon HENRI.

And next day I'd weep and wail and gnash and
    bellow and banshee;
In the evening, for my larynx, I sipped warm and
    honeyed tea,
Then again adjourned, when night returned, to bars
    discerned to be
Fitting haunts for those whose woes bear
    repetition endlessly.

Now I wander ancient alleys in my city by the sea
And I cobbleslip and stumble, often bruising
    buttocks three;
Yes, I have the extra buttock lest two prove
    a paucity,
But'll clutch no more that late adored and ashen
    butt to me.

THE TWA DUNCIES

A bibulous gent
And a simpleton went
Riding out on a pack mule one day

On a mission they'd bred
To dissever the head
From the rest of a man named Fauré.

This Fauré was a rat
Who had offered them that
Morning insults galore to repay

When, with pious reproofs
For the drunk's sodden goofs,
He'd admonished the dullard to say

That he'd no longer lend
His betippling friend
Help in mischief, misdeed, and foul play.

The censorious tone
Of this scolding had sown
Such a hatred for haughty Fauré

That the drunk got an axe
To administer whacks
To his neck 'til his head fell away,

And he gave the dunce chain,
Said Fauré to restrain,
So his arms wouldn't get in the way.

But their mule up and died
When, rehearsing astride
It, the souse let a swing go astray.

Irked, he ordered the fool
To go shove, so the mule
Might stop balking and start to obey.

The fool's feet churned in place
'Til he fell on his face,
Cracked his head open, and passed away,

While the drunkard passed out,
And his gutful of stout
From his innards out wended its way.

When the sozzle came to
He was rattled right through
By the scene that he came to survey,

And completely bereft
Of recall, he was left
To make sense of the gory display.

He climbed sobbing a-lurch
To his feet, and a church
Thereby showed itself just by the way,

So he ran there full-tilt
In the throes of a guilt
That confession, he hoped, might allay.

He'd surprised his old friend
In the act with the end
Of his mule, he informed the curé,

So he'd brained the poor dunce
And had no doubt at once
Recognized he had, to his dismay,

Little choice now, alas,
But to silence his ass
Lest the story come out. Well it may

Have been then that his grief
Had found gushing relief
In cathartic self-soiling. The gray,

Kindly, care-worn old head
Of the priest shook; he shed
A salt tear; and as Father Fauré

Gently chided his friend,
The two wept, and thus ended
A tragically circular day.

JOHNNY PIGASS

Johnny Pigass ate a pie.
A whole one. Someone wondered why
But I thought it made perfect sense:
"He's Johnny Pigass—are you dense?"

ON BEING NYE

Oh why, oh why
Does it appear
That Nye is nigh
When Nye is near?

And why if I may murmur "Nye
Is nowhere nigh" is it the case
That Nye his nighness can't deny
Unless he lay his larynx waste?

And would he further put about
That he's not "Nye"? If deeply shy,
A madman, wanted man, or spy,
Or prey to thoroughgoing doubt

He might. And, pointing further out,
Were I Nye, wouldn't that imply
That, shaving, Nye'd be eye-to-eye
With me, and I with Nye, and we
Could in some sense be said to see
With four eyes? If we postulate
A Nye not I who shaves nearby,
My eyes and Nye's may number eight.

May number eight
By happenstance
Is wheatie M
Dumb A in France,

And M and A and N-Y-E,
When shuffled, spell out "Any me,"
And any me could not but be
Quite close, in point of fact, to I—
Which in itself defines well "nigh."

Links lost on some to some are clear;
To who can delve, the deeps appear;
Chords only chime on strings in tune;
Affinities, like rhymes, lie strewn
To mark the way for who can track;
They yoo-hoo to who yoo-hoo back.

HEREAFTER

Soft I'll recline on satin then
    And study oaken lid,
But I don't think I'll rise again
    Like Jesus did.

Though mulching dark shall cloak my eyes
    And stillness stop each ear,
The eulogists' well-meaning lies
    I might just hear.

Hark, muffled through my boxy bed
    Shall come the mourners' cry:
"He can't be dead! He can't be dead!"
    "Oh yeah?" I'll sigh.

My skin, gone putty-pale, will grow
    As soft as bacon fat,
But I'll still grow some toenail, so
    At least there's that.

I'll molder, bloat with gasses; worse,
    Grow slick as sweaty cheese,
'Til finally my organs burst—
    No pictures, please!

And delving roots shall find my veins
    Right through the casket top—
But are they mine? What rights remain
    When I am slop?

And gnawing worms my head may choose
  As home, each as he dines
Usurping matter I now use
  To write these lines.

O! thin the thread of life that, cut,
  Unravels artlessly
To make the poet consummate
  The consumee!

Who cares if my light verse should charm
  Some one some distant day
When I have long since bought the farm
  And am purée?

And who needs foresight if it shows
  The grave? Why plan ahead
Long range when everybody knows
  Long range we're dead,

With dreams all dreamt and passion spent,
  Bones heaped with promised land,
The happy highways where we went
  Adrift with sand?

And yet we work and scratch and scrape
  As if we hope, in time,
Our steady effort might just make
  Us better slime.

SHOULD BEASTS BE MET

Should you ever meet a grizzly bear
Don't grab him by the testes
For, in spite of his impassive air,
He's easily distressed. He's

Only comfortable alone, has
Trouble interacting, may think
(Though won't say so) that his gonads
Aren't properly your plaything.

And the Bengal tiger likewise may
Be irked to find his phallus
Being grabbed and wrung; who do, display
Bad manners. All such callous

Schadenfreudians shall Luddite-like
Avoid the gnu—phlegmatic
Beasts who stare, when teased, like walleyed pike
Or gaping day-dead haddock.

Although even here—hands off the rear!
There's nothing that surpasses
The shock of the gnu whenever you
Shove oddments up their asses.

In conclusion, please don't blithely tease
A beast who might well mind—who
Might just undertake to firmly make
Your face face toward behind you.

Your reverseward nose would juxtapose
With necknape and backside; you
Could withdraw though, since your fresh footprints,
Now formed in front, would guide you.

THE LITTLE FLOWER GIRL

"Oh please don't buy
What rose ye choose!"
She cries to one who tarries;

"With coins, sir, I
Will but buy booze
And burst more capillaries.

"Nor buy this—smell,
Sir, be my guest—
Last crocus!"—held aquiver—

"The lousy swell
That bought the rest
Is poisoning my liver.

"I'm too inclined
To tipple and
So humbly must implore you,

"Sir, be so kind
And lend no hand
To this poor wretch before you!"

She long kept up
Her loud lament
And then, at break of day, eyed

Her empty cup—
Its testament:
Self-knowledge is no hayride.

SELF-PORTRAIT

I sit before my desk and stare;
Perhaps you wonder whether
I see at all. I'm looking where,
Just out of sight yet just at hand,
The words take shape. I weigh them, and,
With vacant eyes and groping care,
I fit the words together.

I AM BORN

Ah, how much better back where there
Was warmth, and quiet too;
Here I must suck the stinging air
And scream and shit and spew.

When kept from care and snugly curled
In my own inland sea
I little dreamt a thronging world
Outside awaited me,

But then the breach! Why did they bring
Me out of that soft cell
To face this senseless clamoring,
This glaring, hard-edged hell!

The muscle-crunching one-way street
That issued here, alas,
Left me exposed, without retreat
Back through its sealed-up pass
When here they grabbed me by the feet
And slapped me on the ass.

The space splashed open all around
Unsettles me; no more
The perfect peace of being bound
By boundless black. Before,

No messages could find me out,
No phone calls were put through;
Here, every fool bends down to shout
A silly word or two.

Yes thanks, I know you're dada and
I recognize my toes;
I know that that's my hand with which
I'd like to punch your nose;

Yes, lean in, stranger making faces—
Barker for a show
Whose dizzy scenes and madcap paces
You would have me know

Astound, amuse, and can't but top
The peace that they replace—
En garde!—and giant bosoms flop
Unfettered in my face.

No more do I, a rajah, ride
A customized sedan,
But snakelike wriggle side to side
To flee as best I can
That press gang from which none can hide,
The brotherhood of man.

Their concepts—"good," "bad," "early," "late,"
"Near," "distant"—which they use
In systems whereby they can state
What's what and which is whose,
They want you to incorporate
When forming your own views.

But verbal symbols which now bore
Me soon will seem sublime;
The public world which I deplore
Will draw me in, in time,
For I'll forget what was before,
All deep, all dark, all mine.

A MAN CAN DREAM

Your parents' house.
Sleeping street.
Early light.
Twittering birds
—Stop
Reacting to some force unseen,
Unheard, but advancing padfooted through the
    neighborhood,
Swarming every house and tree,
Shimmying the mountain ash to sweep the birds
    flapping from its branches
(They mill and sort and
Whip one nattering circle, and depart);
Climbing, swelling, pushed forward by its own
    rearguard it
Stirs the leaves, makes
Swingsets creak and
Powerlines hum swinging,
And the low-droning force, now fetched up against
    all limits,
Piles back into itself so that
Wave writhes against wave until the very earth
Trembles with its tension, and
From the house where you were raised,
Now vibrating,
Erupt your bathrobed parents running haggard
    and fistapump,
Too terrified for wife-of-Lotlike looks back
As behind them the house creaks,
Lurches,
Slowly turns,
Torques, cracks, splinters,

Roars and flies to pieces
And the thundering earth
Whisks the pieces round,
Opens up,
And corkscrews down.
Your parents are screaming
AAAAAAHH fleeing
The undulation that hill-ripples outward,
Engaging more and more surface as
It spins down into itself,
Slow at the outermost,
Accelerating inward,
Focused on the house-hole lot,
Transforming tumbleclods of earth
Through superagitation
To burbling oatmeal;
O vortex mucilaginous,
Almighty omphalos,
Inswizzling liquefactor,
Your drainsucking force
Now snares the—
Godfrey Daniels!—
Fodderin mudderinlaw,
Feet grabbed so that they must
Robes aflap follow,
Whipping round the eddy loop-a-loop, their
Arms waving high and teeth clenched white,
Beauty queens on a runaway float,
Tug-a-whirl down the oatmeal spout with their
Whipped arms slapping spray off its walls,
Faster and faster,
Tighter and tighter,

Spinning away AAAAaaaaaaaaaaaaaaaa . . .
Until they are lost from sight.

The oatmeal, appeased,
Now glubs and slows;
It congeals to earthclods
And the earthwhirl rises back to flat,
And the spinning dirtclods tumble to a rest,
And the world slows down to stop,
Full stop,
With the peaceful updrift
Of airspeckle dust.

In the neighborhood now leveled
And quiet as a stilled gong,
We listen:

Nothing.

Huh.

For your benefit,
I wipe a tear away.

LAMENT

I doubt if Shakespeare, Sophocles,
Or Keats wrote dipshit lines like these.
With mind so dull and thoughts so small
I wonder I get by at all.

But then, the tufts of verse I sprout
Are never what I had set out
To grow. I think I'm tending seeds
Of rose and rue, and up come—weeds.

SOMETHING FOR EVERYONE

Who rise to adversity,
I shit on you,
But who handle it worse than me
I shit on too.
Who is bright, effervescent,
And shows ready wit
And a cheer that's incessant,
On you I shit.
On the oh-so-refined
I shit; on they
Of wide taste and broad mind,
It's bombs away.
Study, who'd understand me,
This inmost thing
Which at those who can't stand me
I also fling.
Upon swells I discharge an
Unstoppered bowel,
And who dwells on the margin,
Too, I befoul.
On the crab and curmudgeon
Who rise not to hate,
Just to gingery dudgeon—
I defecate.
Thou, sincere, ever wont to
Give praise, not to scoff,
Pardon me if upon you
I pinch one off.
More mature? Then excuse this,
Matured below;
Less mature? You could use this,
My Rapid-Grow.

Who would judge me for all of my
Bile, don't, please,
Before judging my semi-soft
Refugees.
Where Good Fellowship's at I
Bow low and pay
My respects with all that I
Ate yesterday.
On who loves, is loved back,
And with joy has been blessed,
And on lovelorn and sad sack
Do I egest.
Who has been through ordeals
I can't fathom, he
Can now have firsthand feels
Of what's been through me.
Kindness earns from my end my
Warm gutfelt thanks,
My own custom-ground blend, my
Fresh-squeezed hot franks.
Who accepts his own measure
Of trouble and treasure,
Resents not, nor rose to
Success dealing blows to
His brothers in striving,
Is true, not conniving,
And thereby earns others'
Admiring words—
In *my* poem, friend, you're
Festooned with turds.

THE ROAD TO HEAVEN

Once Passion's speeding trap begins
To bounce in Age's ruts,
Straight Virtue's road beats bumpy Sin's;
'Til then, though—hello sluts!

'Til then bring on the sluts, my friend,
The rough and ready sluts;
'Til Old Man Scruple hobbles in,
Step out and sin with sluts.

Since hoovering line after line
Of cocaine makes me nuts
I really should reform some time;
For now, send coke and sluts.

For now, cocaine and sluts, my friend,
Good blow and powdered sluts;
Bring slatterns and cocaine cut fine,
Pure coke and impure sluts.

I gave up liquor long ago,
No ifs or ands or buts,
Except in social settings, so
Bring booze, and coke, and sluts.

Bring booze, cocaine, and sluts, my friend,
Rare substances and sluts;
We'll all the pleasures prove, as though
It rained booze, coke, and sluts.

I wake up with my head aroar
And aching in my guts,
And crabs aromp, and septum sore—
No more booze, coke, or sluts!

No booze, cocaine, or sluts, my friend;
No gargle, buzz, or sluts;
'Tis sin to wait to sin no more
Because of creeping Age when your
Reform can come of gluts;
Who'd virtue court, drink deep, and snort,
And do consort with sluts; commend
Your moral life to sluts; ascend
To saintliness with sluts; attend
The counsel of your nuts; extend
Your private parts to higher ends
Ad maximum with sluts!

BLOOMINGDALES,
OR, ONTOLOGY

The piped-in sound and
Filtered air,
A smell like vinyl everywhere;
With senses dazed and
Minds adrift
Unblinking shoppers tack and shift
Among the shoals of
Merchandise
Or eddy near a lowered price;
Some hold a bag by
Means of string
Which holds a box which holds a thing;
Tread looms on tread, groove
Follows groove
As people move and rise and move;
The escalator
Peters out
Before your floor. Long looks about
Locate the next (though
Not the stair)
Past mannequins with molded hair;
No south no north no fro no to,
No way to look away, the view
Is thronging things, sealed, scented, new;
Phenomenon upon the rack;
The noumenon they keep in back.

CHURCHYARD

The river's rise
He didn't note
And didn't flee,
And didn't float.

Bad judgment but outstanding form:
Three under in a thunderstorm.

A lad of muscles, grace, and vim,
   An able athlete all around
Who with strong strokes could smartly swim
   Almost the whole way cross the sound.

Inspired in us all the hope
That we ourselves not slip on soap.

This earth now checks the baleful stare
   Of gossip and maligner;
You touched us, Teacher, and you shared
   Yourself in ways benign, or
They could have proven you impaired
   The morals of a minor.

Leisure's ardentest martyr: ease
Hardened his arteries.

He loved his youngest, last wife best,
And as their wedding night progressed
His heart skipped one beat, then the rest.
Lord, someone misses him. If not,
His children miss his house and lot
The which his missus now has got.
Beneath these words may he find rest:
Found comfort on a young wife's breast
And, oh, so briefly, in a slot
The mate now fills upon his yacht.

A doughty hunter, spirit bright;
A laugh was ever his response
When friends suggested that he might
Clean shotguns with less nonchalance.

Went caroling
Without a hat,
Gave cheer, caught cold,
And that was that.

He ran back in for the Matisse
That hung above the mantelpiece.
We shuddered, Lord, to hear his screams
As his path met a burning beam's,
And pray his soul is now at peace as,
Hopefully, it's met Matisse's.

Oh, boldly mark my last words, dear:
Engrave how, met with trials,
I sat and faced them without fear—
Don't specify, please, piles.

You've gathered to Your bosom, Lord,
Your servant, whom we all deplored.
Because he roistered hard, and whored,
And subsequently loudly snored,
A bier with no one else aboard
Is ever after his reward.

Caught coatless when it came to pour
He dashed one April day
To make it here to run no more
As of the first of May.

The while she bided with us here
She was attached to someone's ear,
Long holding forth on how to best
Do this or that. Now she's at rest
And, doubtless, with her race now run,
The shades are hearing how it's done.

DOG, DEBONAIR

A dog, debonair,
Stood on two legs and
Gazed along his nose, murmuring,
"I was at a marvelous restaurant last night,
New seafood place downtown called
Daddy's Mallorca.
Strange name;
Wonderful menu though.
Lovely ceviche. Grilled fish. Prawns.
Service—very attentive.
All the food—quite good.
Have You Bean?"
I said,
"Fuck you,
You're just a dog,"
And kicked him and
He scrambled away on four legs yapping.
Ordinarily I feel bad after I kick a dog, but
He asked for it.

RETIREMENT PLAN

Someday I'll set aside my pen
And have the time to practice Zen,
Reflect, read Proust and *Moby Dick*
And Heidegger, and pull my prick.

IF I MAY

If you have sensitive thoughts that you want to put
    in a poem,
Let me tell you something:
Nobody gives a shit.
Whoever invented this idea
That poetry should contain sensitive insights
Has just about ruined the poetry business.
If I read one more poem about emotions,
About what it's like being a man,
Or woman,
Or describing a scene, or time of day, or wordless
    doings between intimates
In a perceptive and sensitive way,
I think I'm gonna puke.
Do me a favor:
If you've thought of a sensitive thing,
Write it down in prose.
Or better yet,
Go fuck yourself.

THE MENTAL GARDEN

O! I love my mental garden;
It's so snug and *sans souci;*
I can sit there sipping cocoa
'Til they wheel me in for tea.

It's a place where pretty birds chirp
And the afternoon sun shines,
And the grillwork on the fence is
Quaintly interlaced with vines.

O! I love it most right after
My electroshock program
When I linger, nodding, trying
To remember who I am.

And I even like the winter
For, although the garden's dead,
In my mind I can imagine
That it's wintertime instead.

O! to find words for its beauty
That the mind can comprehend;
Oftentimes I try to do so
With my nurse for hours on end.

In the spring I sit there drooling,
And I chuckle in the fall;
In the summer I sit screaming
As I face its southern wall.

O! it's soothing of an evening
As the twilight softly spreads,
But it's scary on those days when
I forget to take my meds.

It's a refuge, it's a haven,
It's an Eden, a retreat;
It's an Eden, it's a haven,
It's a refuge; I repeat:

O! I love my mental garden;
It's so snug and free of care
That I think that I shall stay
Until they need my mind elsewhere.

TOPPLED IN THE STREET

I saw a man toppled in the street.
Strangers gathered to look down and say,
"Are you all right?"
He looked at us, frightened, and
A little embarrassed
That his body, after a lifetime of meekly
    obedient service,
Had decided to rise up,
Grab him by the ear,
Make him dance,
Then fling him to the ground, where it was now
    stomping him,
Turning his business suit into a silly costume and
His important errand into farce.
It was showing him who was boss
All right all right,
And in public too.
It made me think of the day,
That humiliating day,
When I myself will topple in the street—
    "HO god . . ."
Will I be alone?
Or will I, perhaps, have been walking with a friend
    or loved one
Who will now run back and forth screaming,
"Help him! Help him! He writes *poems*!"?
I will lie on the sidewalk
Gazing up at the strangers gazing down,
And feel small sidewalk pebbles through the back
    of my head

As I look from side to side,
Head lumpily rolling.

Golly,
I hope I get good strangers.

THE WRESTLER: A FRAGMENT

(From lines composed upon viewing J. Todd Anderson's
    The Naked Man, then forgotten in greater part)

. . . Yet Sarco, look,

Match done, the public's prodding stare
Withdraws, the which he has withstood,
And, now offstage, he comes to wear
The lineaments of childhood
    As through a private gate
He plunges to retrieve his first
    And truest state.

In memory the last ebbs first
And what came early most abides.
The clouds of recent past dispersed,
His dogging shadow no more hides—
    And that persistent mate
Of passing years the wrestler now
    May contemplate.

The shadow tells who is to come;
The destiny was in the lad;
Youth fixed the point; a moving sun
Swept out from it the life he's had;
    The gnomon's outline, Fate,
Has ever limned the days elapsed
    And those in wait.

Hold, Sarco! What commences? Strange!
Such writhing, when no laurel pends!

Nor Past, nor Fate he'll rearrange
And yet, alone, the man contends!
    What dreadful groans!
    What cries! What rage!
The wrestler with himself contends! . . .

I AM FINISHED

I am finished.
Quit fussing with me,
Moving a word here,
Then there,
Then back again,
Changing a line break, a
Comma,
A dash—
Fiddling all my little buttons and snaps,
Wiping my chin,
Matting down my cowlick;
I'm fine the way I am.

Stop looking at me like that.

SOLUTION

"Guns don't kill people;
People do"—
Like all half-truths,
Smug.
Similarly,
"Pens don't write poems;
People do."
A partial truth.
The fact is, if
We took away their pens, their
Pencils, their
Typewriters, their
Word processors which most of them don't
    even understand,
If we broke their fingers,
We could stop the poets. Face it,
Financial penalties don't work.
"Ah," you say, "written poems you
Could stamp out, yes,
But what about oral tradition?
Recital?
Bardic verse?"
I am right there with you, friend.
I cannot abide a bard.
The ridiculous clothing,
The toga,
The silly hair,
Fringe upcombed onto the pate to make
Hair-horns at the corners,
The interminable chanting,
The mournful, oh-it's-tough-to-be-a-bard air,
The annoying lyre plinks—
Yes, the bard is an especial problem.

But,
If you reached in and grabbed his tongue, firmly,
As you must because it will wriggle and dart—
Reflexively, as if it had independent life,
Suggesting that even if the bard wished to cooperate
(Which, believe me, the sonofabitch would not)
His tongue would still evade on its own
Like a fish flushed panicked from behind its
    dental reef—
Grab firmly, as I say,
And pull out to the fullest extent possible,
And saw across with a good sharp knife—
Taking care to cut downwards, not up,
So that when the last stringing stretch of flesh is
    sliced away
And with a wet *fwut!* the tongue pops free,
The knife will not go Yippee! upwards into
    your eye—
If you did this simple,
Simple thing,
The oral tradition too would stop—
Or else turn into an amusing form
More clownlike than bardic.
Truly I say,
With the will,
We could take away those means by which
Bad poets prey upon us.
We would also lose the good poems,
Uh-huh,
Like this one,
But consider:
Good poems, bad—
How many of each?

TO A DEAR LADY

I find in you a certain charm
That others do not seem to see;
Your barking laugh provokes alarm
In some who hear it—not in me;

Your scalpskin's tendency to flake
Recalls those hemispheriform
Tableaux which one may gaily shake
To rouse the settled snow to storm;

And festive too your shock of hair,
Rebuke to who would call you vain;
It can't require too much care—
And how it beckons the insane!

Your buttocks, giant laggards, gray
With slicked-on psoricidal cream,
Are nags whose solemn wobbles say,
"Don't whip us; we're the lady's team."

To me they're lovely as your face
Which, chapped too coarse to crumble cheese
Or polish steel, is squatter's space
For gnawing funguses and fleas—

A flaw to some; to me a sign
Of that same hospitality
That's prompted men to stand in line
To sleep with you for next to free.

The masses merely you embrace,
However, not their trite ideals,
The common ruck esteeming Grace
And Beauty—your Achilles' heels;

Ignore the crowd, though, and you're "strange;"
Who cross the footworn path its groove
Shall tug and try to disarrange;
One stands out, many disapprove.

Their gibes rain down without relent,
But you refuse to take the bait,
Lips ever sealed except to vent
The gasses off of things you ate

—A comeback in two senses. Through
Its sharp deployment you've replied
Succinctly to who, meeting you,
Nod greeting, turn, and run and hide.

I love the challenge others flee;
Your glance entrances me alone;
Another's might firm parts of me,
But yours the whole can turn to stone.

APRIL IS TORNADO SEASON IN MINNESOTA

When at 4:30 in the afternoon the sky turned an
    ass-bruise green
And the wind grew dank and whippy
And the treetops began to suck, bend,
And snap like pennants;
When it grew dark,
So dark
It should have been raining
But wasn't,
But then suddenly did, in cold plump drops
That hit the window and took quivering
    fat-boy steps
Sideways not down across the windowpane;
When the house, our impassive house,
Began to whine, wheeze, whistle, and moan
"Oh dear oh dear oh dear,"
And the dog trotted around the living room,
Tail stiffly wagging but making high whimpers,
A doggy mental case,
Seeking pats of reassurance and then ducking them,
Alarmed that the world had abandoned its plod of
    day and night
For this ghastly in-between,
This cadaver of an out-of-doors come shuddering
    to life
To canter down the street and whip the dashers-
    home-late with
Its damp flapping windings—
Then, as doggy knew but couldn't say,
It was
It was
Tornado Day.

We would observe Tornado Day down in
    the basement,
Holding a transistor radio in its itty
    overalls-like pouch
With sound perforations on the bib and,
Exposed through one shoulder-hole,
A plastic tuning dial
Which we thumbed by its milled edge,
Too fast at first,
Making stations splat between static,
And then slower, to land
On a dry voice reading
Over a steady faraway whoosh:
"Tornado watch in effect
Until eight o'clock
North of a line running from Chaska
To Blue Earth
And south of a line
From Bemidji
To a point twenty miles north
Of Thief River Falls.
Tornado *warning* in effect
West of a line . . ."
Sometimes the announcer would take a call
From a firsthander, thin voice raised
Against the buffeting static:
"Ffffffffffee a funnel cloudffffffffff . . .
Ffffffffftouched down brieflyffffffffffff . . .
Chchchchchtandergar verychchchchch
    shhhhhchchch . . .
Shhhhhhchnoddenkachshchchch . . . "

"Okay, thank you, Don.
For those of you just joining us . . ."

While we listened, we waited
For our own house to start vibrating
Until it, with wood-smashing clamor and shriek of
    wrenching nails,
Would levitate,
And, after hovering pause,
Twirl roaring into the sky—
Us left gawking on
A square of linoleum outlined by
The splintered stubs
Of ripped-away walls.

It never happened.

We never had to go to the next suburb over
To kick stupidly at the pieces of our house drizzled
    across a stranger's lawn;
We were never those poor sad souls on the next
    day's news
In morning-after gym pants and T-shirts,
Squishing through wet grass among ruined effects
Flung and frozen like bodies at Shilo.

A woman in a cat sweatshirt would talk haltingly to
    the camera,
Take two great gulping inhales, goggle, and ram a
    hanky into her face.
Next to her, a man in a feedcap
Grimly squeezed her shoulder.

O YALE MAN

O Yale man,
Would it be all right if I groveled before you and
    smeared myself with your feces,
Or would you prefer that I show by more subtle
    word or sign
That you are my social and intellectual better,
O Yale man?

O Yale man,
Are your sophistication and wit the froth merely
Dancing atop the vasty deep of your
    accomplishment,
And are you secretly amused at the pretensions
    of others,
Secure in the cosseting knowledge that you are a
    Yale man,
A quiet purring pleasure that you harbor
Like a slit-eyed Siamese nestled among your
    intestinal coils (or between perhaps them and
        your pancreas)
Ever humming up your innards, yes oh yes oh yes,
O Yale man?

For you,
O man with lip curled in sneer of Eli,
I wish that I could put into one bottle the
    pussy juice
Of all the beautiful women I have slept with, and
    brandish it in your face, bellowing,
"These are drippings collected from the vaginas of
    women who admired, were attracted to, and
        brought to screaming orgasm by, me,
            a non-Yale-goer,

So much more full than your bottle,
O Yale man!"

I wish that I could dance on your grave,
O Yale man,
And someday shall, singing loud Yale songs in a
    mocking and derisive manner
While you, with your flesh moldering and plopping
    off of your Yale-degree-awarded bones like the
        tenderest osso bucco,
Shall somehow be dimly aware of but powerless to
    silence my belittlement of you and your precious
        status-enhancing institution,
O Yale man!

And then, perhaps, O Yale man,
I shall have you exhumed by court order through
    well-placed bribes,
And when your body has been wheeled into the
    examining room and the indifferent attendants
        have been paid off and withdrawn,
I shall rip the Phi Beta Kappa key from the stiff
    fingers interlaced upon your chest
And shall use it to scoop out your rotting
    eye-jelly and,
After wiping the key on your hair,
Shall climb onto the examining table and squat
    over your head and shit into each eyehole,
And then descend and with the handle of the key
    tamp the outbulging shit firmly into each
        eye socket,
Filling it to the uttermost,
Leaving a Dairy Queen curl atop the protruding
    excess,

And then I shall tell you that I am considering
    applying to Yale for a continuing-education
        course in Yak Fucking,
And shall ask whether you as a Yale man consider
    this one of the stronger parts of the curriculum,
And shall gaze at you staring shit-eyed at the ceiling,
    hugging myself, smiling inly,
Pretending to wait for an answer that I know shall
    never emerge from your shrivellips;
And shall it not be so,
O Yale man?

O Yale man,
Be it so!

REMINDING ME OF SOMEONE WHOSE
BED DOES NOT, AND SON DOES, SPRING OUT

You left me, but I can't escape
    Your trace, abiding in my head
Like Norman Bates's mother's shape
    In Norman Bates's mother's bed.

I still retain, and still resent,
    The press of things you did and said,
Like Norman Bates's mother's dent
    In Norman Bates's mother's bed.

Of old affairs new pain is mint;
    That fullness to this hollow led,
Like Norman Bates's mother's print
    On Norman Bates's mother's bed.

The past reserves its empty spot
    And grins at me, although it's dead,
And Norman Bates's mother's got
    A vacancy—it fills her bed.

YOU WANT SPOOKY?

I'll give you spooky.
It was this dream:
I wake up one morning and my penis is gone.
I look down and it's just not there.
No blood,
No foul play by the looks of it,
My penis is just not there.
Not in the sheets, not in the blankets
(I shake them out to make sure),
Not on the floor next to the bed;
Gone.
G-O-N-E!
I run downstairs to call for help—
And my penis is sitting at the kitchen table,
Calm as you please,
Glasses halfway down its nose,
Drinking coffee and reading the newspaper.
My *balls* were gone too
As I realize when I see them there,
Under my penis,
Bracing it so it can sit upright.
My penis glances at me,
Arching an eyebrow,
And then goes back to reading the newspaper.
I say, "What the fuck is going on?
What are you doing there?
What am I supposed to do without a dick?!"
(My voice cracks a little on "dick?!"),
And the penis just looks up again,
Trace of a smile,
Amused little headshake,
And then goes back to the paper.
I am enraged.

I kick the chair out from under my penis,
Wanting to rattle it,
Wanting to destroy its self-satisfied calm,
And sure enough, when the chair clatters down
And my penis flumps to the floor,
It drops its superior act and squeals and
    skitters away
And disappears through a hole in the baseboard.
I figure Fuck.
Okay.
I lie down flat on the ground and stick my hand in
    the hole,
But here's the weird part:
In spite of the fact that there should be no room,
Or only inches,
Between the interior drywall
And the masonry exterior,
When I reach in
I just keep going
All the way up to my shoulder,
My hand sliding along cool dusty flooring
With nothing in the way.
I grope this way and that,
And still feel nothing—
No masonry, no plumbing, no electrical;
Maybe a few lint balls, but
Certainly no penis.
Then suddenly—*WHAP!*
My penis grabs my wrist
And holds it pinned in there.
And my penis is surprisingly strong.
I cannot move.
I yell, "What is *with* you, penis?
. . . Okay, fine!

If I'm not going anywhere, neither are you!"
But my penis just holds me there,
Arm fully extended inside the hole.

Now this is when
I hear the scratch of a key at the front door;
It jiggles and turns
And the lock clicks free
And the door swings open,
And, OH my GOD,
Two Nazis are walking in.
They wear stormtrooper uniforms
And each has the cold, cold smile of command.
They walk over, jackboots thumping the
    floorboards,
And look down at me, pinned helpless before them.
One says (German accent):
"So, Jew.
You vish to haf your payness back giffen to
    you perhaps?
And yet—I sink not . . . "
And here he's raising his hand.
"Ze payness is mit us now!"
And it's true:
My penis rides up on his hand,
And it also has the cold, cold smile,
And wears a little Nazi uniform
And glinting rimless glasses.
It looks like Heinrich Himmler.
And I'm thinking, Oh no.
Oh my dear God, no.
If the Nazis have my penis—
Who has my arm?

TO A YOUNG WOMAN,
MAIMED BY A REAPER

A clatter flushed you where you were
Reclining in the barley fields;
Your outthrust leg did not deter
The inward-sucking sawtooth wheels;

How gamely you hopped back before
Its limb-enveloping advance;
Its driver's earplugs damped its roar;
He heard nor saw your Lindy dance.

But bad turns worse—for it was Chris,
Your fiancé, who drove, and failed
To notice anything amiss
Until your leg was reaped, and baled.

The ambulance shook you awake,
And Chris, with prefaced "No offense,"
Said cripples bugged him; he must break
It off in yet a further sense.

He wrote, months later, "Wish me well . . .
So sudden . . . soulmates . . . She accepts . . .
A ballerina named Giselle . . .
Do we have acrobatic sex!"

Today how poignantly you hip
And hop upon your prosthesis,
Lamenting that you've had to skip
(No pun intended) wedded bliss,

But, if not yet, perhaps one day
The loss of leg will come to feel
Like not too high a price to pay
For losing such a calloused heel.

I HAVE A DREAM

I sense that something is not right.
"Mm. Something . . . off," I murmur.
I can almost . . . put my . . . finger on it.
—Yes, that's it; pants.

I am not wearing pants.

I am pricked by the suspicion that this is not good.
I am not at my best without pants.
The unease nibbling at mind's edge
Now nickers and rears in terrible certainty:
This is bad.
My heart is squeezed; my face floods red. I realize
That my uncrossed legs leave my crotch exposed—
And my inmost soul vulnerable—
To whatever assaults lurk
In this job interview.

I have *idiotically* robbed myself of the confidence
So crucial in these ego-testing situations.
Not bold assertive panted man—
Offer-muller, alternative-weigher,
    opportunity-considerer—
I am, rather, a hesitating, blushing, umm-er-
    uh-mumbling
Mass of hot and cold flesh,
Inviting judgment,
Shrinking,
Wanting to pile-drive myself into the ground
With repeated fist-blows
To the top of my own head.

How not wear pants.
How not wear pants.
How not wear pants.

The man interviewing me too is uncomfortable,
His pity spiked with anger
At me, blunderer,
Who has foisted upon *him* the role
Of forbearing blunderee.
His pants are smartly creased,
The cuffs proud turkey crops
Waggling over shoes new-shined,
The fly-rippled fabric lying in stiff waves upon
    his crotch
To mask the boisterous contours
Of *his* privates.
Pants:
Good choice; good choice.

Me,
My stockings end in hairy shins,
And my bare thighs bulge pallidly against the chair.
My stupid, *stupid* tighty-whities
Grab at my groin too weakly, I fear,
For will my balls not loll?
It is impossible for me to focus on the
    man's questions:
Even if my genitals do not show, I think,
Their outlined lump
Will look absurd, surely!
Che ridicolo!
Why would I not wear pants?!

And I should have brushed my *teeth*.
My outwafting coffee-breath
Will, won't it, offend this correctly assembled man
    of business
Who can blithely open *his* mouth ungut-racked by
    worry over
Fetid exhale? Darkly,
I wonder about air currents and the distance to
    his nose,
Further distracting myself from the business of
    the interview,
And apply the same anxious calculus
To those farts I cannot stifle,
Wondering whether their thin bleats of protest
Against the leather cushion hemming them in
Are audible to him,
Who farts not.

I also hope that it is a failure to notice,
And not polite affectation of indifference,
That keeps the interviewer from mentioning my
    thumping erection.
I fear that the interview will end before my
    penis subsides
And I shall be forced to rise to shake hands,
Making it unignorable,
And perhaps even prompting it to elbow out of
    its peeflap
Like a neglected party guest jumping unbidden into
    the conversation,
Determined to present his social bona fides.

This would be bad.

The pants would have helped all this stuff.
This social stuff.
I must remember, next time.

Pants.

Pants.

MODEL

I could write an ode on you, my love,
    With your charm its theme and thrust,
Or alleging you're a shrew, my love—
    And both were just.

It could count the happy days, my love,
    That your cheer has brought to pass,
Or enumerate the ways, my love,
    You chap my ass.

Your great grace it might distill, my love,
    In one gesture it recalls,
Or describe with what great skill, my love,
    You bust my balls.

Did its similes and rhymes, my love,
    Place your lips at Virtue's trough,
They could too announce, at times, my love,
    You piss me off.

That your facets form a piece is, love,
    Something verse could only show
If the stanzas came with creases, love,
    To fold just so.

RIDDLE

What has
A howling heart
And lungs that blow across the rattled reed of
    your being
To send flatted sevens down the longest
    steaming street
Of the sultriest city on earth
Where neon slaps GIRLS GIRLS GIRLS onto wet
    pavement in front of
Vast concrete towers whose honeycombed rooms
    contain each one
A man, writhing as he struggles to achieve orgasm,
His moans slipping beneath the door
To join other moans whisping and curling along
    the floor
Toward ever wider hallway junctures
Where still more moans spill out to feed
A great roaring river of lust,
A Big Muddy, a mighty Missouri, an Amazon
Sluggish and strong at the bottom but lashing high
    a tug-tossed foam
Composed of bubbles,
Tiny bubbles,
Each
The evanescent record of one human eruption,
Straining wiggle-walled to burst with merest pip
    or pop,
But together in their million billion pounding the
    atmosphere like a Niagara whose thud and spray
Wave windy mists across the whole of human
    history?

Is it not sex itself, the which you might approach
    and,
Arms hugged to chest, eyes squeezed against its
    salty spume,
Might you shout above its roar: "Sex! O sex! Let me
    feel thy power!
Take me into thy great grabbing current
And wash thundering about mine ears;
Make flail the limbs,
Inflame the mind,
And dash the rocklike self to fine and
    sparkling sand!"?

Or not?

Is sex a wretched thing?
For—to return to the crumbling bordello of
    uncounted rooms—
Shall not each man, having climaxed, sit
    shoulder-sloped
And dully push leg one then two through
    trouserholes
And rise and shake arms into sleeves
Of shirt and coat and overcoat and creaking
    briefcase hoist and trudge away?
And shall he close the door upon
A woman who with legs outslung
Now mops with damp discolored square of cloth
Love-sprung, love-pummeled private parts,
Used washcloth's *thwack* against the wall
The signal for the next in line—
That long, long line of men who stand
And shift and check their watches and, like

Trainawaiters, list and lean,
To prompt the next to further lean,
The whole rippling, centipedelike—
To enter,
Drop his briefcase, shimmy rumpled from
    his clothes,
And clamber aboard wheezing "Dearie dearie
    darling dear"—
Is *that* not sex?
Each orgasm one small dispiriting spurt of energy
Spent to spin a flywheel
That for one brief moment will pulse a tinted
    lightbulb which,
Combined with all other orgasms, concurrent,
    past, succeeding,
Compose the great flashing Las Vegas strip of
    human carnal enterprise,
Scored by Wayne Newton singing "Danke Schoen"?

Unavoidable, though,
Sex;
Even if you pour whiskey into your body
  nd slather its insides with fatty foods and,
    rough lack of excercise and exposure to sun,
      1 it into a pale sluglike thing
        rolls forward, hug-a-muck,
          ing pieces of uptaken dirt from between
          'dering folds of flesh
            1 from grinding tank treads—
                you are caned by the occasional orgasm
                ʾ teeth bared, panting,
                  humping a sofa cushion.

Consider (speaking of the animal kingdom)
The aldridge wark, a small bird of South America
Whose orgasm is so intense
That its shaking will sometimes detach the brain
        from its cranial lining
And literally scramble it, inducing seizures
That end higher function so that the bird, catatonic,
Drops from its perch to the rainforest floor
To be feasted on live by dry scuttling bugs.

If this is sex,
Eyeballs rolling lemon-cherries-bar-cherries
Until the wheels lock and the contraption shudders
        like a washing machine loaded with
            wingtip shoes
And its lid flies open to shoot jingling coin as
        somewhere a parrot shrieks,
"Dawk! Dawk! Pieces of eight!"
Then why do some people talk about "the mystery
        of sex"?
What is so goddamned mysterious about *that*?

And then,
Where does love fit into all this?
I loved a woman once.
We had sex, yes,
And it was all right,
But then we decided to just be friends
And meet once a week and discuss Proust.
And you know what?

THE WISE MAN

He bade me smell each chanced-on rose,
    Or, if I couldn't, quite,
To mine the boogers from my nose
    And flick them where I might.

Quoth he, "Hark! Man is animal,
    So go thou, glut thou, and
Be not much bothered, bowel full,
    With where the leavings land.

"At their first twinge," advised the sage,
    "Dig in and scratch your balls;
Commit no verse to printed page
    Unfit for outhouse walls.

"Convention's crabbed writ decrees
    The end of happy days;
A house respected, pleasure flees;
    Where heads wag, pleasure stays.

"So live your dreams!"—and here he rose
    With fervor to his feet—
"Especially, my child, those
    That end in soiled sheets!"

He turned away; the sands did swirl;
    I never saw him more—
Though how like him the dear, dear girl
    My wife, months later, bore.

HOW LONG, HOW LATE

How long unseen, although, my dear,
Your youth survived in every dream
—The which is why, new met, I fear
   I started somewhat, biting back a scream.

How sobering to think that you
Surveyed one equally antique
—The which is why, reflection true,
   You started also, stifling a shriek.

How lullingly the days file by
Until we see their number weight
A once familiar face, and cry,
   "I've been asleep! How late it is—how late!"

I DREAMED I LEFT MY KNAPSACK

I dreamed I left my knapsack on the subway.
It had my things, all my things,
The things with which I earn my living,
Things useless to others,
Making sense only to me—
Paper with information on it,
Calendars, organizers, and
Electronic contrivances
By means of which I marshal all the little tricks
    and dodges
That exploit my few strengths and hide my
    many weaknesses;
All those things that help me
Operate in, and protect myself from,
This hard, hard world.
As the doors finished closing and the
Big metal train trundled away,
I stood on the platform feeling weak,
And reflected, walking home, without its familiar
    weight upon my back,
That there was no replacing my knapsack,
No way to simply carry on as before;
Now I would be chasing after the loose strands of
    my business,
Head whipping this way and that, hands
Furiously waving as if herding skittish sheep,
Trying to coax my affairs forward knapsackless
While at the same time engaged in a rearguard
    attempt
To re-create its contents.

I sank lower and lower,
Mentally rummaging the vanished bag's
    compartments,
Ticking off the irreplaceable things inside,
Each remembered item another piece of armor
    clattering to the sidewalk about me,
So that,
By the time I got home and managed to close the
    door behind me,
I had turned into a soft quivering snail,
No longer human and,
Lacking shell,
Not even identifiable among the monopods.
I sat gelatinously on the floor, trembling with dread,
Until my wife, my beloved wife, came down
    the stairs
And saw me.
She shrieked, of course.
I tried to tell her who I was
But managed only to make soft cheeping sounds, my
Palps undulating pathetically toward her.
She shrieked anew and grabbed our little boy's
    shovel.
As she chased me around the kitchen
I wanted to say,
"Yes, dear, there's little left of what I was, it's true,
But this part is the inmost me,
My quaking heart;
Do not recoil from it, from me, o beloved wife."
It came out soft cheeps.
I slithered in the space between cupboard and floor,
Toy shovel banging after me and
My beloved wife's shrieks ringing about me.

One whack caught my flesh, slicing out a divot that
The shovel blade's backward flick slapped against
    the metal face of the dishwasher;
It dribbled down leaving a trail of slime.
This slowed me, and the shovel hit me again,
And again,
Slicing me,
Smashing me,
Spattering the new wood facing of the lower
    kitchen cabinets
With snail gore,
And I was thinking, and it was my last conscious
    thought,
Better this,
Maybe,
Better the children remember me as a strong
    smiling man,
Hoisting them high,
Heartily laughing,
Striding out into the world to beat it on its terms,
Than that they learn I am a slug
Getting mashed into the tile floor of the kitchen
    with a small metal spade.

Later—and I don't know how I know this—
My wife pants, trying to collect herself,
Hair hanging about her face.
She rises from her knees,
Walks dull-eyed to the sink,
And runs hot water over our dear little boy's shovel.
She dumps it clanking into its pail,
Rolls up her sleeves,
Fills a plastic tub with hot, soapy water,

Waves the back of her hand at a whisp of hair that
    clings to her sweat-beaded forehead,
And starts scrubbing me off the kitchen floor.
Much much later—the next day, in fact—
She will answer the door to
Luis, a good man of the boroughs,
Who holds my knapsack, saying,
Your address was inside;
Does it belong to you, ma'am, or your husband?
My husband?
Her eyes are far away.
My husband?
It sounds familiar, a name she can't quite place . . .

I DREAMT I SAW ST. AUGUSTINE

I dreamt I saw St. Augustine
Who asked me how the hell I'd been.
The deity, he said, said Hi,
And all the saints had asked if I
Would drop by to belt back a few.
The martyrs wished, he added, to
Know how it hung—but this is when
I woke up, stretched, felt for my pen,
   Wrote down my dream,
   Ate some ice cream,
Belched twice, and went to sleep again.

ABOUT THE AUTHOR

Ethan Coen lives outside of Marfa, Texas, on the ranch he won arm wrestling Lady Bird Johnson in a cantina in Ensenada in 1962 (the ensuing love story was celebrated in his memoir *Don't Tell Lyndon*). He is an expert on the poetry of Walter Savage Landor and many other subjects which he travels the world to lecture upon, unsolicited. Coen is Poet-in-Residence at the University of Big Bend and hosted its "Fire in the John" poetry readings until they changed the open bar policy. Under the pen name G. Willard Snunt, Coen is the author of the Moe Grabinsky mystery stories, detailing the adventures of the wily toll-taker/sleuth. In his spare time he is shot from cannons.